The idea for this sixty-mile route was inspired by the well documented 13th century journeys of King John between Windsor and Winchester via the Castle he built near Odiham. A straight line drawn on the map joins these three historic places, with Odiham exactly half-way. While many aspects of the countryside have altered dramatically in the 800 years since John's time, the contours are unchanged and we can still use some of the old ways that he would have known. Today, we pass through a variety of attractive scenery – parkland and forest, over heaths and downland, beside quiet streams and through picturesque villages.

EASY TO FOLLOW

Despite recent development, we can follow a continuous chain of rights of way. With the addition of some permitted paths through Crown Estate woodland, we are able to complete our journey, using less than five miles of mainly unclassified roads. The route has good rail connections at the start, middle and end. (See last page for a map and travel information.)

PLAN AHEAD

Plan your walk perhaps over five days. If you are a regular walker, three stages a day (12 miles) – or even more with light evenings – would be possible. Try to allow time to explore Windsor and Winchester, as both have so much to offer the visitor. What gear you take depends very much on the season but walking boots and waterproofs are always advisable. Keep to a minimum what you carry but be sure to plan ahead. For example, note that between Greywell and Itchen Abbas (a distance of 22 miles) there is only one small shop and one public house actually on the route. You will need a copy of our WHERE TO STAY leaflet. (See over page.)

N ...
A ...
C ...
h ...
t ...
published in 1992 but the route is not specially way-marked as we consider this unnecessary. Disregard signs indicating other 'named' routes which sometimes coincide with the Three Castles Path. As this edition goes to press, all the paths are clear and usable but if you find any problems, or have ideas for improvements, you can help other walkers by contacting the Local Authorities concerned.

Look out for the special postcards!

AN INVITATION

This is not a strenuous walk - don't let the gradient profile (shown after Stage 15) put you off. There are few steep hills to climb, not that many stiles and rarely much mud! We suggest this is an ideal 'first long walk' and are confident it will provide much quiet pleasure and a great sense of achievement to those who take up the challenge.

CIRCULAR WALKS

Six short circular walks have been included as an introduction to the area through which our linear route passes.

Symbols: ⊖ Bus Stop   🅿 Car Park   P.H. Public House   ❸ Link with circular walk
          🅒 Public Convenience   ☎ Telephone   𝒊 Information Centre

WINDSOR
The Castle
Open daily from 10.00
Admission £9.50 (includes State
Apartments). Tel: (01753) 868286
The Great Park
Open during daylight hours.
Large groups of walkers (15/20 or more)
should contact the Crown Estate Office
beforehand. Tel: (01753) 860222

ASCOT
The Heath and Racecourse
To prevent any rights of way being
established the Heath is closed to the
public on the first Tuesday every
November. Racing takes place on about
24 days each year. Tel: (01344) 622211
*On race days golf is not played, so it is
safe to use a very old route known as
Church Path running straight across the
Heath towards an avenue of very tall
Wellingtonia trees.*

ODIHAM
The Pest House
Cared for and maintained by the
Odiham Society.
Usually open Saturdays and Sundays
throughout the year. 10.30–16.00
Admission free – donations welcomed.
The Castle Ruins
Cared for and maintained by Hampshire
County Council.
Usually open at all times.
Admission free.

WINCHESTER
The Cathedral
Open daily 09.00–1700
Admission free – donations welcomed.
Tel: (01962) 866854
The Great Hall
Open: Daily   10.00–17.00
        Sat/Sun Nov–Feb 10.00–16.00
Tel: (01962) 846476
The Hospital of St Cross
Open: Summer 09.30–17.00
        Winter 10.30–15.30
Closed Sundays.
Admission: £2
Tel: (01962) 851375

WHERE TO STAY
A leaflet prepared by the East Berks RA
Group, giving the latest information on
Bed & Breakfast Accommodation for
walkers along the route is obtainable by
sending an SAE to:
Tourist Information Centre
The Look Out, Nine Mile Ride,
Bracknell, Berkshire RG12 7QW

TOURIST INFORMATION CENTRES
Windsor
24 High Street, Windsor, Berkshire SL4 1LH
Tel: (01753) 743900
May–Sept   Mon–Sat   09.30–17.30
                Sun   10.00–16.00
Oct–April   Daily   10.00–16.00

The Look Out
Nine Mile Ride, Bracknell,
Berkshire RG12 7QW
Tel: (01344) 868222
Open daily: 10.00–17.00
Cafe. Viewing tower & 'hands on'
science exhibition (charge).

Basingstoke
(Stages 6–11)
TIC, The Willis Museum, Market Place,
Basingstoke, Hampshire RG21 7QD
Tel: (01256) 817618

Winchester
The Guildhall, Broadway, Winchester,
Hampshire SO23 9LJ
Tel: (01962) 840500
May–Sept   Mon–Sat   10.00–18.00
                Sun   11.00–14.00
Oct–April   Mon–Sat   10.00–17.00
Closed Sundays.

*The information given above is believed to be
correct at time of publication.*

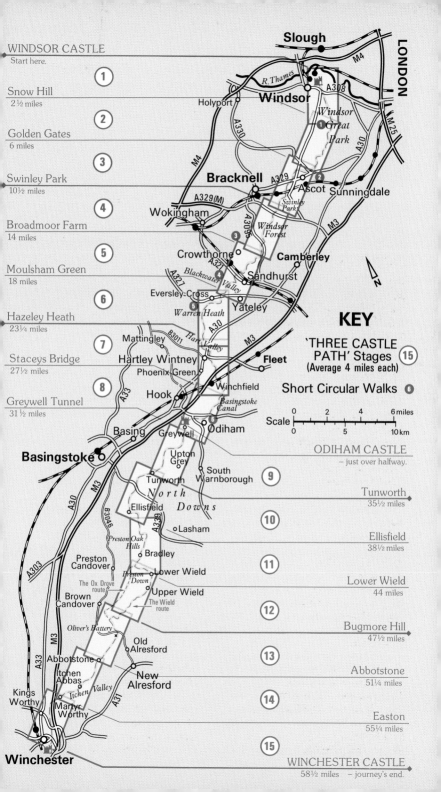

WINDSOR CASTLE
Start here.

①

Snow Hill
2 ½ miles

②

Golden Gates
6 miles

③

Swinley Park
10 ½ miles

④

Broadmoor Farm
14 miles

⑤

Moulsham Green
18 miles

⑥

Hazeley Heath
23 ¼ miles

⑦

Staceys Bridge
27 ½ miles

⑧

Greywell Tunnel
31 ½ miles

Slough

LONDON

R. Thames

M4

A308

Windsor

Holyport

Windsor Great Park

A330

A30

M25

❶

A329

Bracknell

A329(M)

A308

Wokingham

A309

Swinley Park

Ascot

❷

Sunningdale

Windsor Forest

M3

A322

Crowthorne

Camberley

A321

Blackwater Valley

❸

❹

Sandhurst

Eversley Cross

Yateley

❺

Warren Heath

Hart Valley

B3011

Mattingley

M3

Fleet

Hartley Wintney

Phoenix Green

Winchfield

Hook

Basingstoke Canal

A33

Greywell

❻

Odiham

Basing

Upton Grey

Basingstoke

Tunworth

South Warnborough

North Downs

Ellisfield

Lasham

B3046

Preston Oak Hills

A339

A30

M3

N

KEY

'THREE CASTLE PATH' Stages
(Average 4 miles each) ⑮

Short Circular Walks ⑥

ODIHAM CASTLE
– just over halfway.

Scale	0	2	4	6 miles
	0	5	10 km	

⑨

Tunworth
35 ½ miles

⑩

Ellisfield
38 ½ miles

Bradley

Preston Candover

Preston Down

Lower Wield

⑪

Lower Wield
44 miles

The Ox Drove route

Upper Wield

Brown Candover

The Wield route

⑫

Bugmore Hill
47 ½ miles

Oliver's Battery

A303

M3

A33

Old Alresford

⑬

Abbotstone
51 ¼ miles

Abbotstone

Itchen Abbas

New Alresford

Kings Worthy

Itchen Valley

A31

Martyr Worthy

⑭

Easton
55 ¼ miles

Winchester

⑮

WINCHESTER CASTLE
58 ½ miles – journey's end.

Windsor Castle and The Long Walk   *Photo: Unichrome*

Windsor Castle has been a Royal residence for some 900 years, longer than any other still in use. Today it is the largest inhabited castle in the world. King John is said to have loved Windsor 'beyond all others'. Until the devastating fire in the State Apartments on 20 November 1992, a fitting start to our journey was the modest tower in the Upper Ward which bears his name (built 1363, much altered since).

Today, the Castle's high entry charge may preclude this. Instead, imagine King John and his knights riding down from the Keep of this commanding site, with mainly wooden defences at that time, and across the drawbridge where King Henry VIII's Gateway now stands.

1 Having admired this splendid portal, (the exit for visitors today), built by Henry and bearing his arms and Tudor badges above the arch, walk straight across Castle Hill into Church St (where Nell Gwynn once lived).

This area of charming cobbled and flagstoned streets is at the heart of old Windsor, or New Windsor as it was called when William the Conqueror first built his castle here.

2 So, as a preamble to our Royal Route to Winchester, walk 'round the block'. At the end of Church St turn right facing the Court Jester, then sharp right up Market St Within a few paces, by the Carpenters Arms, turn left into Queen Charlotte St, claimed to be the shortest in Britain. On the left stands, or rather leans, the quaintly lopsided Market Cross House. Then turn left between the Portland stone arches of the imposing Guildhall.

Notice the four columns beneath, but not quite touching, the floor of the Banqueting Hall above. When the architect Sir Thomas Fitch died soon after building had begun in 1687, supervision of the work was taken over by Sir Christopher Wren. At the request of the townspeople who doubted, it is said, the strength of the design, Sir Christopher inserted these columns. Three centuries later the four-inch gaps remain!

3 Shortly pass the Parish Church of St John the Baptist on left, then bear left into Park St and if so inclined, take the last opportunity of refreshment for some miles, at the Two Brewers, by Park Street Gate.

Until it was closed in 1851, Park Street continued straight across the Long Walk to Old Windsor. At that time

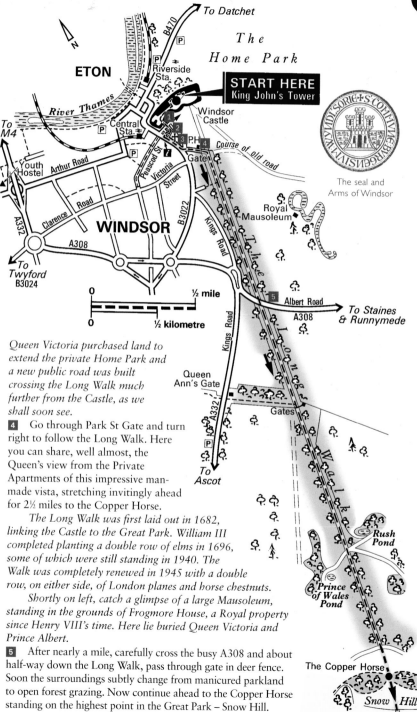

To Datchet

The Home Park

ETON

Riverside Sta.

START HERE
King John's Tower

River Thames

Windsor Castle

To M4

Central Sta.

P.H.

Park St Gate

Course of old road

The seal and Arms of Windsor

Youth Hostel

Arthur Road

Peascod St

Victoria Street

Royal Mausoleum

Clarence Road

WINDSOR

B3022

Kings Road

A308

To Twyford B3024

0 ½ mile

0 ½ kilometre

5 Albert Road

A308

To Staines & Runnymede

Kings Road

Queen Ann's Gate

A332

Gates

To Ascot

The Long Walk

Rush Pond

Prince of Wales Pond

The Copper Horse

Snow Hill

Queen Victoria purchased land to extend the private Home Park and a new public road was built crossing the Long Walk much further from the Castle, as we shall soon see.

4 Go through Park St Gate and turn right to follow the Long Walk. Here you can share, well almost, the Queen's view from the Private Apartments of this impressive man-made vista, stretching invitingly ahead for 2½ miles to the Copper Horse.

The Long Walk was first laid out in 1682, linking the Castle to the Great Park. William III completed planting a double row of elms in 1696, some of which were still standing in 1940. The Walk was completely renewed in 1945 with a double row, on either side, of London planes and horse chestnuts.

Shortly on left, catch a glimpse of a large Mausoleum, standing in the grounds of Frogmore House, a Royal property since Henry VIII's time. Here lie buried Queen Victoria and Prince Albert.

5 After nearly a mile, carefully cross the busy A308 and about half-way down the Long Walk, pass through gate in deer fence. Soon the surroundings subtly change from manicured parkland to open forest grazing. Now continue ahead to the Copper Horse standing on the highest point in the Great Park – Snow Hill.

The commanding bronze statue of George III (known as the Copper Horse), was erected by George IV, in honour of 'the best of fathers'. Sculpted by Richard Westmacott, the 30ft high granite base is modelled on a monument to Peter the Great, in St Petersburg. It is said that before raising the statue in 1831, '16 men got inside, had a luncheon of bread and cheese, drank the King's health and sang God Save the King'.

The Great Park today, although covering 4,800 acres, is only a remnant of Windsor Forest; at one time it included large parts of Surrey and all of east Berkshire. Much of the Park is open to the public on foot and includes many interesting features, such as Virginia Water, Savill Gardens, Valley Gardens, Smith's Lawn, etc. Overall it is an area of great natural beauty and tranquillity, cared for and much loved by successive Monarchs from 1129, when the first 'Parker' was appointed, to his counterpart today, the Ranger – HRH Prince Philip.

1 Pass the Copper Horse and continue in same direction. Soon a wide mown strip leads down to another gate in the deer fence and a wide grass ride with low hedges either side. After a crossing ride, look left for glimpse of Royal Lodge, a favourite country retreat of the Queen Mother's since she and the then Duke of York first moved there in 1934. At end of ride with woodland ahead, continue on rising gravel track (note Ox Pond close by on right), to reach junction of Park roadways. Here turn sharp right, past Chaplain's Lodge on left. At fork in road bear left, with fine views sweeping down ahead. At road crossing turn left, to pass The Hollies on left and to follow Duke's Lane, lined by many fine old oaks – notice plaque: 'Planted about 1751'.

2 Leave the Great Park by Prince Consort's Gate and continue along lane, soon to reach public road (B383) at Ascot Gate. Turn right along grass verge for 60 yards, then cross road to enter, by self-closing 'Rambler's gate', a tree-lined path between fields of Sunninghill Park. *This path replaces a right of way through Home Farm, visible away to right, site of a house built in 1990 for the present Duke of York.*

3 The path soon widens into a track. At T-junction turn left onto concrete drive, soon becoming tarmac. Where drive starts to bear right, a short diversion to visit Great Pond is possible by turning right onto narrow winding woodland

The Royal Procession at Ascot Gate

The Copper Horse

path, crossing wooden footbridge over stream, leading to the pond.

4 Retracing your steps, continue to end of drive at East Lodge and then turn right along footway (Cheapside Rd).

The white painted gates shortly on right are used by the procession of landaus conveying HM The Queen and her party, as it drives onto the course each day of the Royal Ascot race meeting in June. Soon you may see through the trees the twin lodges and ornamental Norfolk Gates (1955), marking the beginning of the New Straight Mile course.

5 Where the road forks by Silwood Park Nurseries, bear left, shortly to reach the impressive Golden Gates. At end of railings to left of gates, turn right into enclosed path beside racecourse.

The Golden Gates and adjoining Lodge (a listed building), were erected in 1879 at the start of the original straight mile course, which is no longer used for racing, partly because it is out of sight from the stands. During the last war wires were stretched across the course along here, between concrete posts, to prevent enemy planes from landing. You may notice a surviving post beside the path.

Follow side of course and at junction, turn right along road (A330 Winkfield Rd). Cross lines of both old and new Straight Miles, then immediately turn left between white posts.

If racing is in progress you may be held up for a few minutes on the road or crossing the course, but there is free public access to Ascot Heath even on race days. This world-famous course was first laid out in 1711 on the orders of Queen Anne who, like her present day namesake the Princess Royal, was an enthusiastic horse-woman, keeping a pack of Buckhounds at nearby Swinley Bottom.

Waiting to cross the course

1 Within a few yards of the road, bear right in front of golf clubhouse to gate in wire fence and through gap in running-rails, to cross the lush turf of two tracks. Turn right along tarmac road, then presently at junction, branch off half-left along narrower service drive – to cross golf course with care. Pass cricket pavilion on right, then cross golf fairway and then racecourse to reach road (A322).

2 Cross into Kennel Avenue (lined with fine Wellingtonias) and in front of Huntsman's House, turn left into Burleigh Rd (Queen Anne's Buckhounds were kennelled near here). Follow footway on right until, just beyond modern houses, Burleigh Rd turns left and so do we. At top of slope, shortly before road junction, turn right into byway (Blythewood Lane), keeping to old track, descending until it finally reaches main road (A329).

3 Here turn right; then just after Gainsborough Drive cross main road via traffic island. Follow verge and turn left

at gate into Englemere Pond Local Nature Reserve. Facing pond, turn right along way-marked woodland path, with pond close on left. Keep left after storage yard and at crossing path (with car park just to right), continue ahead to stile at road (Swinley Rd), opposite Whitmore Cottages.

4 Cross road, turning left, over railway. At bottom of slope turn right into Swinley Park, part of the Crown Estate. Shortly, at junction of forest rides, turn sharp left along broad grass ride, and follow Permitted Path sign, the first of several over the next 1½ miles. Where drive from left merges (Windsor Ride) continue ahead, now on tarmac, and at top of rise stay on drive turning right.

About 300 yards beyond this bend, notice immediately to right, a semicircle of 12 old lime trees which probably marked the turning circle for carriages bringing Royal hunting parties in the 18th century from Windsor Castle to Swinley Lodge, which stood nearby until about 1825. Some of the trees here and elsewhere in the Park show traces of a shield and the letters 'WF' (Windsor Forest) carved on the trunks, denoting

Swinley Park

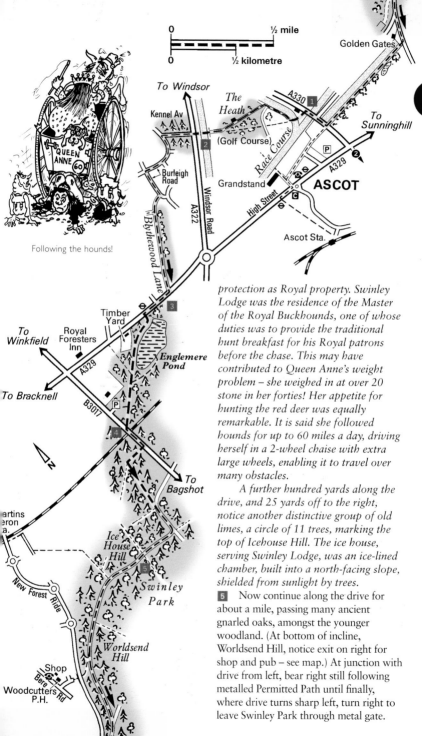

Following the hounds!

0 ½ mile
0 ½ kilometre

To Windsor

The Heath
(Golf Course)

Kennel Av

Golden Gates

To Sunninghill

A330 **1**

Race Course

Burleigh Road

Grandstand

ASCOT

A329 **2**

P

High Street

Windsor Road

A322

Ascot Sta.

Blythewood Lane

Timber Yard

3

To Winkfield

Royal Foresters Inn

A329

Englemere Pond

To Bracknell

B3017

P

4

N

To Bagshot

artins
eron
a.

Ice House Hill

5

Swinley Park

New Forest Ride

Worldsend Hill

Shop
Bere
Woodcutters P.H.
Rd

protection as Royal property. Swinley Lodge was the residence of the Master of the Royal Buckhounds, one of whose duties was to provide the traditional hunt breakfast for his Royal patrons before the chase. This may have contributed to Queen Anne's weight problem – she weighed in at over 20 stone in her forties! Her appetite for hunting the red deer was equally remarkable. It is said she followed hounds for up to 60 miles a day, driving herself in a 2-wheel chaise with extra large wheels, enabling it to travel over many obstacles.

A further hundred yards along the drive, and 25 yards off to the right, notice another distinctive group of old limes, a circle of 11 trees, marking the top of Icehouse Hill. The ice house, serving Swinley Lodge, was an ice-lined chamber, built into a north-facing slope, shielded from sunlight by trees.

5 Now continue along the drive for about a mile, passing many ancient gnarled oaks, amongst the younger woodland. (At bottom of incline, Worldsend Hill, notice exit on right for shop and pub – see map.) At junction with drive from left, bear right still following metalled Permitted Path until finally, where drive turns sharp left, turn right to leave Swinley Park through metal gate.

From Swinley Park turn left along roadside verge (New Forest Ride). Just beyond roundabout cross road using traffic island and continue in same direction along pavement. At next roundabout footway bears right to access footbridge spanning dual carriageway (A322). Pass Coral Reef swimming pool on right and 25 yards past car park entrance, turn left to carefully cross road (Nine Mile Ride B3430). Follow entrance drive through car park to main buildings of the Look Out.

SPECIAL NOTE: Although Broadmoor Hospital is 3 miles away, hereabouts you may hear the alarm at 10 am on a Monday morning. Don't worry – they're just testing!

The Look Out was opened by HM the Queen in April 1991, together with public access to a series of walks, trails and rides through some 2,600 acres of Windsor Forest. This is very much a 'working forest', producing some 15,000 tons of timber each year, mainly Scots Pine, for use as sawn logs, fencing material, telegraph poles and pulp for paper-making. The unusual viewing tower is fast being overtaken by the growing trees!

1   Walk to left of the Look Out, past picnic area, and go half-right on broad path, then bear left, marked 'Heritage Trail', and keep straight up this rising sandy track. Where Heritage Trail turns right, go straight on up incline until, at next crossing track, with bank on right, turn right. After 100 yards bear left onto wide ride (grass at last!) Continue ahead at next crossing (Ladies Mile) and on reaching T-junction turn left (Heritage Trail again) soon to reach and turn right along a more prominent track, The Devil's Highway.

This is the route of the Roman road from London to Silchester (via Staines), so-called, it is said, by the tribes that lived here after the Romans went home, because they thought only the Devil could have built a road so straight!

In this area are the remains of several military redoubts – raised banks

Refreshments and events at the Look Out

Suspension footbridge over dual carriageway

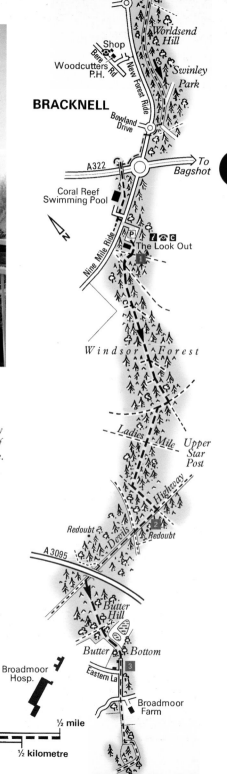

with outer ditches. *These were built about 1792 for training purposes, against the threat of possible invasion by Napoleon's forces, and were the scene of large-scale military exercises at that time.*

2 Follow grass strip beside the gravel Highway to a 'Ramblers gate', then continue ahead along undulating track to finally pass under bypass (A3095). Then, at end of fence on left, turn left along path, soon reaching tree-covered slopes of Butter Hill and down past the (inaccessible) ponds at Butter Bottom.

3 After 'Ramblers gate' near cottage on right, continue on road, becoming Eastern Lane, with views of Broadmoor Hospital away to right. *Built in 1863, it is a special hospital for psychiatric patients under secure conditions. As mentioned earlier, the alarm system is tested at 10 am on Monday mornings!* Where road turns right, keep straight on over stile by metal gate to pass the buildings of Broadmoor Farm on left.

Broadmoor Farm to Moulsham Green 4 miles

Leaving Broadmoor Farm follow path ahead through two fields with wire fence on right, turning left and right through woodland, finally to cross stile and turn right along delightful tree-lined avenue. At stile cross road, to go ahead up bank between posts into light woodland with green metal fence on left. After stile near houses, continue to far end of woodland, cross ditch and turn left through V-stile beside gate.

This area is Owlsmoor Bog and, shortly, Edgbarrow Woods, an SSSI covering 78 acres – one of the few remaining heathlands in Berkshire. There are some rare plants, birds and insects to be found here.

1 Follow fence on left and at crossing turn right on path now running parallel with overhead cables away to left. After metal gate ahead continue to end of woodland. Carefully cross road (Crowthorne Rd), to take path bearing left between metal posts, down through trees and under cables. Stay on slowly descending sandy path which joins broad track, to end of woodland where properties appear on left and then houses on right. This is Sandy Lane and you have reached Little Sandhurst, which boasts at time of writing two pubs, two general stores and a Post Office.

2 Notice Fox & Hounds on left (corner of Hancombe Rd) and 120 yards further down lane, immediately after No. 13 Woodfall, turn right down tarmac path. At bottom turn left (Grampian Rd) and then right (Chiltern Rd). Round left-hand bend, at No. 33, turn right on path between houses, to bear left into woodland ahead. Follow path with wire fence on left, then just before open field turn left through metal swing-gates and carefully cross railway line to enter National Trust woodland, Ambarrow Hill. (For details see Ramble 4.)

3 Within 50 yards of the railway turn left through fence gap into grounds of one-time Victorian mansion, Ambarrow Court, now a Country Park. On reaching tarmac path turn right and follow left and right bends to reach car park. Carefully cross road (A321) and pass via stile-way onto path along edge of woodland strip. Joining road ahead, within a few yards turn left into field through swing-gate. Follow ditch along edge of two fields, with buildings of former Ambarrow Farm away on right. At end of second field cross lane with kissing gates either side into meadow

Near Broadmoor Farm

where gravel path leads ahead through a water sports centre (Horseshoe Lake).

4 Beyond the launching area stay on gravel path, finally bearing right in front of one swing-gate, to shortly reach a second. Here turn right along path beside Blackwater River, the boundary between Berkshire and Hampshire.

You are now in the Blackwater Valley, which extends for some 12 miles between Eversley and Aldershot, along the Hampshire border with Berkshire and Surrey. The path has been created as the result of 'planning gain' linked with the extraction of gravel. Beyond Horseshoe Lake are three more lakes forming a nature reserve of some 90 acres. Special planting and landscaping has encouraged wildfowl and wader species. Two public viewing hides have been provided.

Butter Bottom

Broadmoor Hospital

Broadmoor Farm

CROWTHORNE

Pine Hill

Owlsmoor

Bog.

Rackstraw Road

A 3095

To Camberley

School

Edgbarrow Woods

P

Edgbarrow Hill

Crowthorne Road

Crowthorne Sta.

To Wokingham

Sandy Lane

Grampian Road

Fox & Hounds P.H.

Shop & P.O.

Little Sandhurst

3

Cheviot Rd

Shop

P

Ambarrow Court

4

Ambarrow Farm

A 321

To Sandhurst & Camberley

0 ½ mile

0 ½ kilometre

BERKSHIRE

Bird Hide

4 P

Mill Lane

Blackwater River

HAMPSHIRE

Moulsham Green

Moulsham Copse La.

Vicarage Road

YATELEY

A 327

Follow the riverside path for nearly a mile but at end of Horseshoe Lake be sure to turn left through swing-gate to stay beside the river. On reaching wooden bridge, cross the Blackwater into Hampshire and take left fork through stile-way into woodland. Path soon widens, then shortly divides, the footpath now between bridleway and lake. At end of lake, ~~exit through gate on right, then~~ continue ahead along gravel path to reach road at Moulsham Green.

At Moulsham Green turn right along road, cross Blaire Park, and turn right along edge of green. Facing properties, turn right then left on drive and enter narrow tarmac path to left of house No. 23 ahead. Cross two minor roads and at metal rails keep right, shortly to cross wooden footbridge and stile. Follow left side of small triangular field and at far corner bear left, shortly turning right, to enter field on left by stile near metal gate. Follow right-hand side of field, passing buildings of Watmore Farm. Cross stile in corner and turn left along Fox Lane, leading to main road (A327).

1 Immediately cross road, turning left, and within a few yards turn right over ditch to follow right-hand side of two fields to reach road with large house ahead (Firgrove Manor). Turn right along road, carefully cross Marsh Lane (B3016), soon to reach the hamlet of Up Green.

The group of three Victorian Gothic cottages facing you at road junction (and three more in the district) were built around 1899, regardless of expense it would seem, by one John Martineau as a memorial to the famous writer Charles Kingsley, who was vicar of nearby Eversley. They must be the grandest labourers' dwellings ever built!

2 Now turn right along Chequers Lane and within a few paces, immediately after

Relief portrait of Charles Kingsley

Reed Field, turn left along tarmac drive between houses. At end of gardens cross stile to follow path, enclosed at first, later open to field, keeping woodland (Lower Eversley Copse) on left. Pass to left of green metal gate into narrow path now with fence on right. Finally at end of large field, cross sleeper bridge and stile, then continue ahead for about 35 yards. Here turn left along side of large meadow, with trees on left. At top of this field cross stile beside gate and immediately turn right along fence on right. Cross two more stiles to reach road. Go straight across green ahead and join lane, passing the Old Manor and St Mary's Church on right. (See Ramble 5)

3 Continue past the Old Rectory to end of lane. Immediately after unusual gateposts, turn left to follow rising path, marking the beginning of the Forestry Commission's Warren Heath, part of Bramshill Forest. Emerging from canopy of tall trees bear left onto wide path, with plantation (of Corsican Pines – planted 1974) on right. Soon the way bends slightly right to reach prominent junction of several tracks.

Besides allowing additional free public access on foot, the Forestry Commission has agreements which provide for more esoteric pursuits here such as horse-riding, carriage-driving, motor-rallying, and dog-sledding – although not all at once!

4 Go straight ahead (across Welsh Drive) to follow wide 'haul route', after noticing concrete pillar on right, (the gravel industry giving itself a pat on the back!). At next crossing (Sir Richard's Ride) continue ahead along curving route.

After the area on the left had been excavated for gravel and hoggin, it was reclaimed for tree planting, using a newly developed 'ridge and furrow' technique. The area was back-filled with top-soil and silt and then ridged, instead of being levelled as in the past. The result is a dramatic improvement in survival and growth of the young trees.

5 Follow this track until, at top of rise and just before it descends steeply

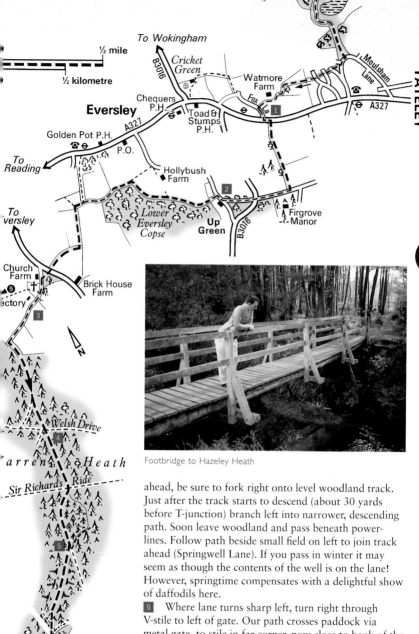

To Wokingham

Cricket Green

Eversley

Watmore Farm

Chequers P.H.

Fox

Toad & Stumps P.H.

Golden Pot P.H.

P.O.

Hollybush Farm

YATELEY

Moulsham Lane

A327

To Reading

A327

To Eversley

Lower Eversley Copse

Up Green

B3016

Firgrove Manor

Church Farm

Brick House Farm

Rectory

Welsh Drive

Warren Heath

Sir Richards Ride

Springwell Lane

Hulfords Lane

A30

River Hart

Hares La.

White Lyon P.H.

Hartfordbridge

Hazeley Heath

½ mile

½ kilometre

Footbridge to Hazeley Heath

ahead, be sure to fork right onto level woodland track. Just after the track starts to descend (about 30 yards before T-junction) branch left into narrower, descending path. Soon leave woodland and pass beneath power-lines. Follow path beside small field on left to join track ahead (Springwell Lane). If you pass in winter it may seem as though the contents of the well is on the lane! However, springtime compensates with a delightful show of daffodils here.

6 Where lane turns sharp left, turn right through V-stile to left of gate. Our path crosses paddock via metal gate, to stile in far corner, now close to bank of the charming River Hart. A pair of stiles and a sleeper bridge carry our path as it continues along bottom edge of next field. A further stile leads into a meadow where path seems needlessly fenced. Cross stream by sturdy wooden footbridge and after 50 yards in trees emerge on Hazeley Heath.

Facing Hazeley Heath, turn left and follow path which passes along edge of heath at first, before winding through the trees with field away to left. Where path rises steeply take the central, steepest route. Emerging from trees, turn left along broad gravel path, now with woodland on left.

1 At end of broad track, where paths meet at clearing, continue ahead on the main path into mature woodland. Winding path descends gradually, passes through swing-gate, soon becoming a roadway past houses on right, finally to reach road (Hunts Common). Turn right along the green and at the end cross main road (A30) with great care and maybe some difficulty!

2 Enter Park Corner Rd with golf course on left, leading to green and duck pond with picture-book Causeway Farm beyond.

Having admired the ducks, turn right through middle of green, following line of oaks. Cross minor road to follow grass verge between cricket green and, naturally, the Cricketers. *Cricket has been played here for over two hundred years.* Cross another minor road and maintain same direction ahead, soon to reach and carefully cross A323 into Green Lane opposite. Follow footway until, immediately after St John's Church, turn left. At end of railings take middle path ahead through open trees (the Mildmay Oaks), to reach road by drive to Vicarage.

The rows of mature oak trees, which are such a feature of the open greens running through the middle of Hartley Wintney, were planted after the Napoleonic Wars for patriotic reasons, by the then Lady of the Manor, Lady Mildmay. The speedy development of iron and steel naval vessels meant that the oaks were spared.

3 Continue along the footway, soon bearing right into Church Lane. Just before a turning (Cottage Green) cross road to grass verge fronting house, Meadow Way. After kissing gate follow field path beside hedge, cross house drive, and continue into next field to enter burial ground adjoining St Mary's Church.

4 Turn left in burial ground and follow the path around three sides of the churchyard, to enjoy the splendid views over what were once the common fields of the medieval village. Just after small brick building exit left through V-stile and on through woodland strip, beside lane. Opposite entrance to Church House Farm, turn left over stile and down through field. Cross drive, then footbridge ahead into field, to follow headland with hedge on left. Cross stile

The Basingstoke Canal

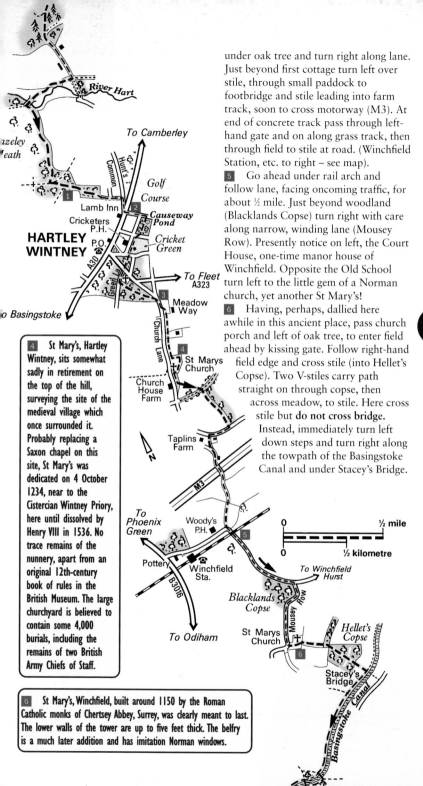

under oak tree and turn right along lane. Just beyond first cottage turn left over stile, through small paddock to footbridge and stile leading into farm track, soon to cross motorway (M3). At end of concrete track pass through left-hand gate and on along grass track, then through field to stile at road. (Winchfield Station, etc. to right – see map).

5   Go ahead under rail arch and follow lane, facing oncoming traffic, for about ½ mile. Just beyond woodland (Blacklands Copse) turn right with care along narrow, winding lane (Mousey Row). Presently notice on left, the Court House, one-time manor house of Winchfield. Opposite the Old School turn left to the little gem of a Norman church, yet another St Mary's!

6   Having, perhaps, dallied here awhile in this ancient place, pass church porch and left of oak tree, to enter field ahead by kissing gate. Follow right-hand field edge and cross stile (into Hellet's Copse). Two V-stiles carry path straight on through copse, then across meadow, to stile. Here cross stile but **do not cross bridge.** Instead, immediately turn left down steps and turn right along the towpath of the Basingstoke Canal and under Stacey's Bridge.

7

4   St Mary's, Hartley Wintney, sits somewhat sadly in retirement on the top of the hill, surveying the site of the medieval village which once surrounded it. Probably replacing a Saxon chapel on this site, St Mary's was dedicated on 4 October 1234, near to the Cistercian Wintney Priory, here until dissolved by Henry VIII in 1536. No trace remains of the nunnery, apart from an original 12th-century book of rules in the British Museum. The large churchyard is believed to contain some 4,000 burials, including the remains of two British Army Chiefs of Staff.

6   St Mary's, Winchfield, built around 1150 by the Roman Catholic monks of Chertsey Abbey, Surrey, was clearly meant to last. The lower walls of the tower are up to five feet thick. The belfry is a much later addition and has imitation Norman windows.

Map labels:

River Hart

To Camberley

azeley Heath

Golf Course

Hunt's Common

Lamb Inn

Cricketers P.H.

HARTLEY WINTNEY

P.O.

A30

Causeway Pond

Cricket Green

To Fleet A323

o Basingstoke

Green Lane

Meadow Way

Church Lane

St Marys Church

Church House Farm

Taplins Farm

N

M3

To Phoenix Green

Woody's P.H.

Pottery

Winchfield Sta.

B3016

To Odiham

0   ½ mile

0   ½ kilometre

To Winchfield Hurst

Blacklands Copse

Mousey Row

Hellet's Copse

St Marys Church

Stacey's Bridge

Basingstoke Canal

The 200-year-old Basingstoke Canal originally ran 37 miles from Basingstoke to the Wey Navigation at Byfleet, to carry farm produce, timber and chalk to London Docks, returning with coal and fertilizer. It was never a commercial success, only being kept afloat as it were, in Victorian times by carrying construction materials for the railways and the military camp at Aldershot. The last barge moored at Basingstoke Wharf in 1910. Today, ownership is shared between Surrey and Hampshire County Councils. Restoration for leisure purposes began in 1973 – officially re-opened May 1991.

Archaeologist David Allen with rounded malmstone, used as seige catapult ammunition

1 Our route now follows the canal towpath for about 4½ miles to the tunnel at Greywell, with possible detours en route. Try the high-level path on the opposite bank between the third bridge (Sprat's Hatch) and the fourth. Returning to towpath look to right (after end of woodland on opposite bank) for small lake, Wilks Water. A short distance around it stands King John's Hunting Lodge (NT but not open to the public). Further along, at Colt Hill, is the Water Witch – a canal-side pub – also access to Odiham. By next road bridge over canal are the Swan pub and a garage with shop.

2 Then, just beyond swing-bridge, across the field immediately to right, catch your first glimpse of the ruined keep of King John's Castle, halfway point on our journey!

Since Saxon times Odiham had been a Royal manor, no doubt a convenient resting place between Windsor and Winchester, being a day's journey from each. With discontent amongst the English barons and the threat of a French invasion, King John chose Odiham as a site for one of four new castles. Between 1207 and 1214, at the 'enormous' cost of £1100, John built a stronghold and a home.

The central feature, the remains of which we see today, was an unusual octagonal three-storeyed tower. Its walls

of flint were ten feet thick, with wide buttresses. The 20-acre site was carefully chosen within a loop of the Whitewater River. The marsh and water-meadows between the moat and the river could be easily flooded in times of danger. This was put to the test, successfully, in 1216 when a handful of the King's men – 3 knights, 3 squires and 7 men-at-arms were confronted by an army led by Louis, son of the French King. This small garrison held out for 15 days

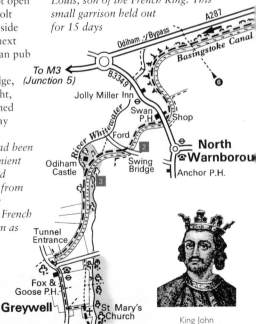

King John
(1199-1216)

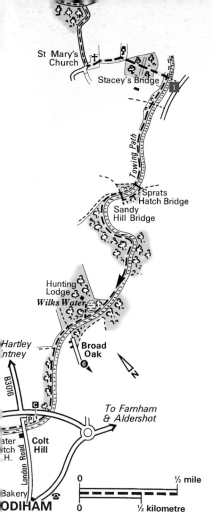

before surrendering, on condition that they retained their freedom, their horses and their arms.

After King John died, Odiham Castle and the surrounding Royal Park continued to provide excellent deer-hunting for his successors. Eleanor, his youngest daughter, inherited the Manor and lived here for 30 years with her second husband, the influential baron, Simon de Montfort.

Detailed household accounts have survived and provide some fascinating information about life in those days. For instance, on 17 March 1265, 1,000 plates were bought for 6s8d! In 1321 some £248 was spent, which included the purchase of no less than 95,350 roof tiles, 3,000 'stones' and 17 tons of lead.

Although no traces remain today, many buildings were constructed in and around the Castle during those years, to accommodate the often large numbers of men and horses who had to be housed from time to time. On one occasion, 334 horses were stabled here or grazing in the nearby meadows.

Castles prolonged wars, but didn't finish them. As the decades went by, the kings and no doubt their queens, wanted greater comfort than the ageing Castle could provide. Also, the importance of Winchester was declining in the 1400s which lessened the usefulness of Odiham.

Although we associate the Castle mainly with King John, it was used at some time by every English king of the 13th and 14th centuries. As we gaze today at the crumbling tower, nearly 800 years after it was first built, it is still a potent reminder of the once vibrant and successful medieval fortress which played a prominent part for more than 250 years through a turbulent period of English history.

We can only wonder whether it was a fine summer's day when, on 15 June 1215, King John rode out of the Castle and turned his horse towards Runnymede, and the Magna Carta which awaited him.

3 Back on the towpath, just beyond the Castle ruins, the River Whitewater flows under the canal. A 'winding hole' nearby, enables barges to turn around before Greywell Tunnel, now ½ mile ahead.

KING JOHN AT ODIHAM CASTLE

Previous Place	1215	Subsequent Place
Winchester	May 21–22	Windsor
Winchester	May 24–25	Reading
Reading	May 28–30	Windsor
Windsor	June 4	Winchester
Winchester	June 9	Windsor
Windsor	June 26	Winchester

The Greywell Tunnel (1125 m) was a long way for the bargemen who had to 'leg it' from end to end. The steps down the bank here enable us, with care, to peer into the gloom beyond the grill covering the tunnel entrance. In 1932 the roof collapsed some 140 ft below Greywell Hill. As a result, the draught-free dark interior maintains a constant temperature of 10 °C (50 °F), providing a perfect environment for the estimated 2,000 bats which hibernate here, monitored by English Nature.

The River Whitewater at Greywell

1 Follow path over tunnel entrance to roadside. Turn right, then left at T-junction, to pass Fox & Goose, and on along The Street.

On right, notice the large timbered wisteria-clad building, the Malt House, originally called Kiln House due to the two hop kilns forming one end. The house is Elizabethan and the wisteria is reputed to be over 150 years old.

2 Immediately before Church Cottage ahead, turn left through lych-gate leading to St Mary's Church in its idyllic riverside setting.

Church Cottage is possibly older than the Malt House, also timber-framed with brick infilling. It is thought to have been the priest's lodging and is said to be haunted.

St Mary the Virgin, like many village churches we admire today, has ancient origins and yet owes much of its appearance to later centuries. In this instance, from its Norman doorways (notice the one bricked up on the south side) to the chancel, rebuilt in 1870 with flint facing and stone quoins (corner stones). The walls of the nave and tower are both 12th century. Inside, an interesting feature is the 16th-century carved oak rood screen.

At church porch turn right past tower and large oak tree to leave churchyard. Shortly, follow raised wooden walkway (built by Hampshire Recreation at our suggestion) to reach grassy bank of Whitewater and, soon, delightful old Greywell Mill. At this point our route turns right, away from the river, but do first follow path to left of waterwheel to view the mill pond in its tranquil setting.

It is rather sad to think that after a mill of some sort has stood here for over a thousand years, since Saxon times, it was only about sixty-five years ago that milling literally 'ground to a halt'. The remains of the old breastshot wheel can be seen, where the weight of water from Mill Head continues to pour down, as though striving to turn once more the now paddle-less wheel. In 1933 the mill was brought to a standstill by a mechanical fault which was never repaired.

The last miller here, one Donald Jabez Dean, then turned his hand to growing watercress for Covent Garden and continued to live in this idyllic spot for over fifty years. (Max Bygrave once made a film here, but you won't want to know about that!)

The Whitewater continues to flow on, to join the Loddon, leaving the old mill to slumber peacefully in retirement. How many millers' daughters may have dallied on this riverbank in a thousand years?

3 Retrace your steps from pond and follow track away from mill. After gate, and 25 yards before junction with road, turn left over stile, then right, to follow field edge, using stiles to keep hedge and road (Upton Grey Rd) on right. This path climbs slowly to reveal extensive views across this western end of the

North Downs. Continue to follow hedge, then fence, through large fields, eventually to reach stile into crossing track – summer route of the historic Harrow Way – at Four Lanes End. Turn right and cross Upton Grey Rd, to follow the Harrow Way with fields on right and trees on left. The Way shortly crosses a shallow valley, leading to a group of fine old beech trees marking Five Lanes End.

[4] From this isolated meeting of ancient tracks, turn left. Just after Dutch barn on right, a Roman road once crossed our path – difficult to imagine, perhaps, in this remote spot. Where surfaced track swings right, keep straight on, along grassy track, eventually to reach road.

[5] Turn right along open road. Pass Tunworth Hill Cottages, descend hill and go ahead at crossroads. Notice Old Post Office cottage and the one-time schoolmaster's cottage with schoolroom attached. Soon bend in lane reveals sweeping entrance to Old Rectory. To visit the tucked-away little church of All Saints, look out for gate at end of white picket fence on left. A line of old beech trees leads to the church past the walls of Manor Farm. Returning to lane, turn left to pass Manor Farm.

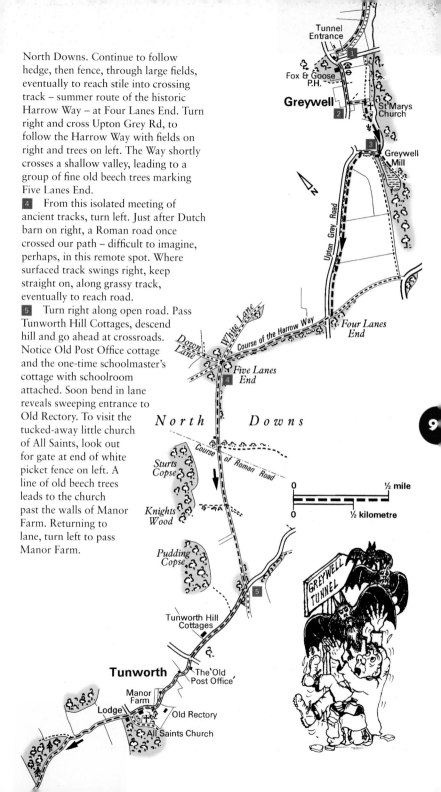

Tunnel Entrance

Fox & Goose P.H.

Greywell

St Marys Church

Greywell Mill

Upton Grey Road

White Lane

Dozen Lane

Course of the Harrow Way

Four Lanes End

Five Lanes End

North   Downs

Course of Roman Road

Sturts Copse

Knights Wood

Pudding Copse

½ mile

½ kilometre

Tunworth Hill Cottages

Tunworth

The 'Old Post Office'

Manor Farm

Lodge

Old Rectory

All Saints Church

GREYWELL TUNNEL

9

After Manor Farm on left, when lane bends right, go straight ahead on this clear bridleway between hedges and fields for about a mile, skirting Hackwood Park estate on right, finally to reach Winslade Farm. Follow farm drive to main road, A339. Here turn left along verge and shortly cross road with care to fork right along track in front of solitary cottage.

The substantial embankment ahead carried the Basingstoke & Alton Light Railway from 1901 to 1936. It was never a viable enterprise; the 12-mile journey took nearly an hour, so it was almost as quick to go by pony and trap! Beyond arch notice isolated one-time Methodist chapel tucked away to right.

1 Where track reaches gateway, go straight ahead into field and follow bridleway beside fence (Whinkneys Copse), to leave field through bridle gate. Maintain same direction through area of young trees to join grass ride sloping up towards open field. Now continue on broad headland with woodland (Allwood Copse) on right. At junction with track going right into woodland, keep straight on along narrow bridleway, still close to same field but now in light woodland. This winding path straightens into a hollow tree-lined track (Alley Lane), and reaches, rather surprisingly, the highest point of our journey to Winchester, 646 feet. Eventually the way widens before reaching road at Ellisfield.

(To visit the one village pub, the Fox, about ½ mile away, turn right here and take the footpath from just beyond the church, across the fields to the south – see map.)

The villagers describe Ellisfield as 'heaven on earth' – and who would argue. Hopefully you will have time to sample some of its delights. Turn right along Church Lane and view the duck pond through the 'hole in the wall', by the Old Manor. The pond wall was built in 1939 by General Nesbit, which was NOT a popular idea at the time!

On the right along here is the Memorial Hall and then Church Cottage (the one-time Post Office). The hall has been the centre of social activity since it was opened in 1920. Can you imagine U.S. servicemen, in full battle-dress, dancing here with the local girls before decamping from the village to take part in the D-Day Normandy landings? The troops were 'under canvas' on Preston Oak Hills, which our route crosses.

The village takes its name - once Aelle's Field - from King Aelle who landed in Sussex in 477 AD. But the Church of St Martin is rather more modern, celebrating its 700th anniversary not long ago. Long before the church was built, what is now Church Lane was the preferred winter (high ground) route of that ancient track the Harrow Way, which we encountered at Four Lanes End.

Footpath to Tunworth Church

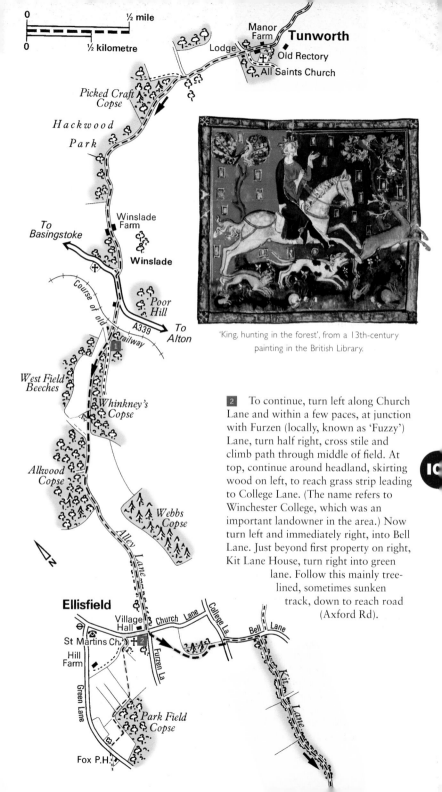

0 _____ ½ mile
0 _____ ½ kilometre

Tunworth
Manor Farm
Lodge
Old Rectory
All Saints Church

Picked Craft Copse

Hackwood Park

To Basingstoke

Winslade Farm
Winslade

Course of old railway

Poor Hill
A339
To Alton

West Field Beeches

Whinkney's Copse

Allwood Copse

Webbs Copse

Alley Lane

Ellisfield
Village Hall
Church Lane
St Martins Ch.
College La.
Bell Lane
Furzen La.
Hill Farm
Green Lane
Park Field Copse
Fox P.H.
Kit Lane

'King, hunting in the forest', from a 13th-century painting in the British Library.

2 To continue, turn left along Church Lane and within a few paces, at junction with Furzen (locally, known as 'Fuzzy') Lane, turn half right, cross stile and climb path through middle of field. At top, continue around headland, skirting wood on left, to reach grass strip leading to College Lane. (The name refers to Winchester College, which was an important landowner in the area.) Now turn left and immediately right, into Bell Lane. Just beyond first property on right, Kit Lane House, turn right into green lane. Follow this mainly tree-lined, sometimes sunken track, down to reach road (Axford Rd).

IC

From the end of Kit Lane carefully cross road ahead (Axford Rd) and 20 yards to left turn up a path created specially for our route. This rises through woodland (Preston Oak Hills), with field nearby on left. At junction at top of hill, turn left along bridleway to road. Here turn right and within a few yards left (Spain Lane), with row of fine beech trees on left. At end of beeches, turn right along broad grassy track, with hedge on left at first. This easygoing path takes us downhill for about 1½ miles, threading its way between woods and fields until, eventually, the appearance on left of a pretty thatched cottage heralds our arrival at the hamlet of Bradley.

1 At this point there is a choice of routes; either along the Ox Drove (see panel on facing page), or the more varied way, described below, through the attractive villages of Bradley, Lower and Upper Wield.

Turn left along lane into Bradley, following right-hand bend to pass neat village duck pond. At this point, look back to see the small flint-faced church of All Saints, perched on the nearby slopes.

This tiny village experienced some notoriety when King Charles I claimed the Manor to settle a debt of £1001.1s. The occupier, one Thomas Taylor,

refused to give possession and for several months held out against various attempts to take it by modest force. Finally, in early 1630, the aptly named Sheriff, Sir Henry Wallop, sent to London for the 'great guns' and with a force of 200 men, destroyed the house. Exit Thomas Taylor!

2 Follow road round left-hand bend, beside garden of Pond Cottage, (almost hidden beneath its thatch), then turn right up track, becoming wide grass path through avenue of sycamore trees. This leads on to a broad grass headland, with large open field on left. Follow hedgerow trees on right for a distance, to reach top of rise (Preston Down). Descend towards valley ahead and half-way down the edge of this field, turn left through middle of it towards right-hand side of woodland ahead (Park Copse). Then, with wood close -by on left, continue on to find swing-gate in narrow corner of field.

3 From swing-gate bear right across end of copse for about 100 yards to stile. From here, cross the large field towards point about half way along cable on horizon. On far side path continues ahead, cutting across two small plantations and track between, then on over the next field to corner of

Hampshire thatcher Adrian Hall completes a cottage roof at Lower Wield

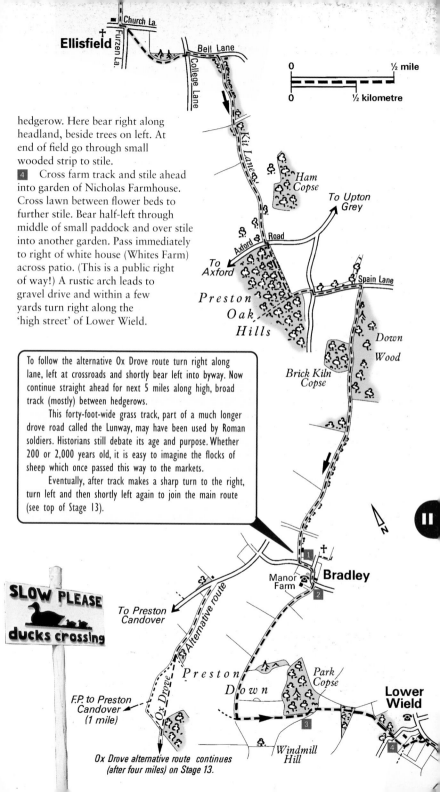

hedgerow. Here bear right along headland, beside trees on left. At end of field go through small wooded strip to stile.

4 Cross farm track and stile ahead into garden of Nicholas Farmhouse. Cross lawn between flower beds to further stile. Bear half-left through middle of small paddock and over stile into another garden. Pass immediately to right of white house (Whites Farm) across patio. (This is a public right of way!) A rustic arch leads to gravel drive and within a few yards turn right along the 'high street' of Lower Wield.

To follow the alternative Ox Drove route turn right along lane, left at crossroads and shortly bear left into byway. Now continue straight ahead for next 5 miles along high, broad track (mostly) between hedgerows.

This forty-foot-wide grass track, part of a much longer drove road called the Lunway, may have been used by Roman soldiers. Historians still debate its age and purpose. Whether 200 or 2,000 years old, it is easy to imagine the flocks of sheep which once passed this way to the markets.

Eventually, after track makes a sharp turn to the right, turn left and then shortly left again to join the main route (see top of Stage 13).

Ellisfield
Church La.
Furzen La.
College Lane
Bell Lane
Kit Lane
Ham Copse
To Upton Grey
Axford Road
To Axford
Spain Lane
Preston Oak Hills
Down Wood
Brick Kiln Copse

½ mile
½ kilometre

SLOW PLEASE
ducks crossing

To Preston Candover

Alternative route

Ox Drove

F.P. to Preston Candover (1 mile)

Preston Down

Park Copse

Lower Wield

Manor Farm
Bradley

Windmill Hill

N

Ox Drove alternative route continues (after four miles) on Stage 13.

On reaching metalled road at Lower Wield turn right to pass several cottages including The Windmill, (a one-time inn of this name). Where lane turns right, continue ahead through garden to reach entrance into field. Descend mid-field path, bearing right, to stile on far side and, within a few yards, to lane.

On the right here is the delightful Yew Tree Inn. The original cottage – the part next to the even older yew tree – was built beside a chalk pit some 300 years ago. By the 1850's it was a beer-house, and now today it is an attractive pub/restaurant, saved from extinction, like many a country inn, by the motor car.

1 To continue, cross lane and go straight up headland path, catching glimpses of cricket field and, later, valley through trees on right. At end of large field on left cross stile and bear slightly left, heading towards cluster of taller trees on far side. Here follow path between hedges soon leading to Upper Wield village green, after passing on left the former school, now the village hall. Stay on right of green, towards thatched cottages.

On our right as we cross the green stands Wield House (early 19th century). Only the porch remains of the previous house on this site, built in 1580/85 by William Wallop, one-time MP, twice Mayor of Southampton,

whose family connection with the area stretches from Saxon times to the present day. Imagine the scene, one day in 1591, when Queen Elizabeth I and her household, forming a great procession, arrived here to take refreshment, no doubt, en route from the Marquis of Winchester's house at Abbotstone, to stay with Sir Henry Wallop, William's brother, at Farleigh Wallop.

2 At this point our route continues straight ahead through the village but the old church certainly merits a visit, so on the far side of the green cross road and take first turning right. Just after Church Cottage on left, with village stores ahead, turn left into churchyard.

St James contains a fine memorial to William Wallop (and his third wife), Wield's most famous son. The church was built about 1150 at the direction of the Conqueror's grandson, Henry de Blois, Bishop of Winchester and is a fine example of a small Norman church of that period. It was probably thatched in earlier days, and until 1810 had a tower, which was found to be unsafe. This was replaced by the present wooden belfry to house the one surviving bell, two others having been sold to help pay for the repairs. The interior is full of interesting features, like the 12/13th-century Purbeck marble font, installed here in 1900,

Wield Church

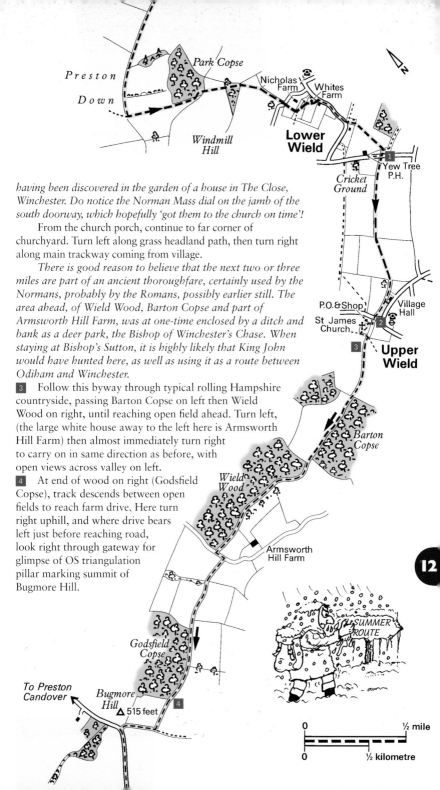

Preston Down

Park Copse

Nicholas Farm

Whites Farm

Lower Wield

Windmill Hill

Yew Tree P.H.

Cricket Ground

P.O.&Shop

St James Church

Village Hall

Upper Wield

Barton Copse

Wield Wood

Armsworth Hill Farm

Godsfield Copse

Bugmore Hill △ 515 feet

To Preston Candover

SUMMER ROUTE

having been discovered in the garden of a house in The Close, Winchester. Do notice the Norman Mass dial on the jamb of the south doorway, which hopefully 'got them to the church on time'!

From the church porch, continue to far corner of churchyard. Turn left along grass headland path, then turn right along main trackway coming from village.

There is good reason to believe that the next two or three miles are part of an ancient thoroughfare, certainly used by the Normans, probably by the Romans, possibly earlier still. The area ahead, of Wield Wood, Barton Copse and part of Armsworth Hill Farm, was at one-time enclosed by a ditch and bank as a deer park, the Bishop of Winchester's Chase. When staying at Bishop's Sutton, it is highly likely that King John would have hunted here, as well as using it as a route between Odiham and Winchester.

3 Follow this byway through typical rolling Hampshire countryside, passing Barton Copse on left then Wield Wood on right, until reaching open field ahead. Turn left, (the large white house away to the left here is Armsworth Hill Farm) then almost immediately turn right to carry on in same direction as before, with open views across valley on left.

4 At end of wood on right (Godsfield Copse), track descends between open fields to reach farm drive. Here turn right uphill, and where drive bears left just before reaching road, look right through gateway for glimpse of OS triangulation pillar marking summit of Bugmore Hill.

12

0 ½ mile

0 ½ kilometre

Bugmore Hill to Abbotstone   3¾ miles

Where farm drive meets road, turn left down hill. At bottom of slope go 30 yards beyond end of field on right before turning right onto track which climbs through middle of broad woodland strip. After admiring the view from top of hill continue along fenced track winding through plantation (Spy Bush) finally to emerge at T-junction. On turning left along roadway (Spybush Lane), we rejoin our alternative route via The Ox Drove.

For the next three miles we also share the Wayfarer's Walk, -which runs for 70 miles from Emsworth on the coast to Inkpen on the Berkshire Downs.

1 Where drive turns right to (Swarraton Farm) go straight ahead, over wooded hilltop, descending by grassy track to reach Oliver's Battery, *(a relatively modern name for an iron-age hill fort site)*, on Abbotstone Down. Cross road (B3046) and, after passing parking area, continue along gravel track. Where this swings right, keep straight on across grassy strip, soon with wire fence on left. Path narrows through edge of Sheep Wood and then continues with hedge on left, open fields to right. Signpost just

before isolated farm buildings shows evidence, for the first time, of our destination - 'Footpath to Winchester'!

2 Continue ahead on track, still with hedge on left until, with buildings ahead (Abbotstone Farm), at junction with track descending from right, bear left downhill.

This almost empty landscape conceals a lively past. The valley ahead was the meeting point of several important routes from Saxon times to the later Middle Ages. To our right, Abbotstone Farm was the hillside site chosen by William Paulet, 1st Marquis of Winchester, for the timber-framed mansion he built in the 16th century. Was it the situation or the hospitality which brought Queen Elizabeth I here, from Winchester, on three separate occasions?

By the late 1600's the Tudor house was in disrepair. In 1685, Charles Paulet, 6th Marquis of Winchester (soon to become 1st Duke of Bolton) started to build a great new brick mansion, just above the old house. The writer, Daniel Defoe, described 'a very handsome, beautiful palace'. The Duke died in 1699 and the house was never finished.

Straight on, over Itchen Stoke Down

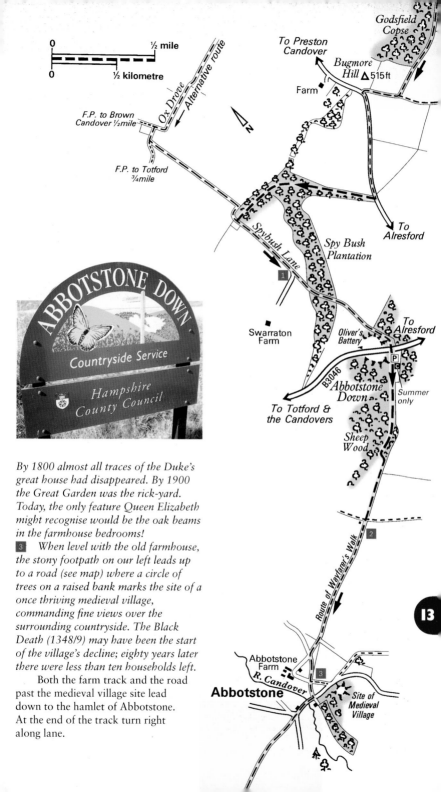

Map labels

0 ½ mile
0 ½ kilometre

Godsfield
Copse

To Preston
Candover

Bugmore
Hill △ 515 ft

Farm

Ox Drove

Alternative route

F.P. to Brown
Candover ½ mile

F.P. to Totford
¾ mile

N

Spybush Lane

Spy Bush
Plantation

To
Alresford

1

Swarraton
Farm

Oliver's
Battery

To
Alresford

B3046

P

Abbotstone
Down

Summer
only

To Totford &
the Candovers

Sheep
Wood

Route of Wayfarer's Walk

2

13

Abbotstone
Farm

R. Candover

Abbotstone

3

Site of
Medieval
Village

By 1800 almost all traces of the Duke's
great house had disappeared. By 1900
the Great Garden was the rick-yard.
Today, the only feature Queen Elizabeth
might recognise would be the oak beams
in the farmhouse bedrooms!

3   When level with the old farmhouse,
the stony footpath on our left leads up
to a road (see map) where a circle of
trees on a raised bank marks the site of a
once thriving medieval village,
commanding fine views over the
surrounding countryside. The Black
Death (1348/9) may have been the start
of the village's decline; eighty years later
there were less than ten households left.

Both the farm track and the road
past the medieval village site lead
down to the hamlet of Abbotstone.
At the end of the track turn right
along lane.

Follow the lane over a stream – the Candover – with cottage on right. Where road divides go straight on into hedged track, its antiquity suggested by the width and steep sides. Five tracks meet at top of hill ahead where we go straight on, over Itchen Stoke Down. *This was once open downland. It became very famous 1770 – 95 as the venue for some historic cricket matches played here for high stakes, as much as 500 and 1000 guineas.* Now continue on narrower, grassy path for a mile to reach road, shortly after crossing bridge of one-time railway.

1 *This line, closed in 1973, once linked Alton to the main line at Winchester. The section between Alton and Alresford has been preserved as a steam railway, the Watercress Line.*

2 Turn right along road for 20 yards, then right again over stile and climb meadow, following line of mature trees round left-hand turn at field corner. Leave field by gate and join short estate road. Turn right at lane ahead and after some 50 yards turn left up bank to follow narrow hedged path, leading to estate road. Here turn right on footway, soon passing Itchen Abbas Primary School on left. At bottom of slope turn left and shortly left again at main road (B3047). Dependent on your inclination and the time of day, either continue ahead for a few yards to the Trout Inn, or cross road at bus stop and fork right towards Avington, to reach lych-gate of St John's Church.

Author Charles Kingsley (see Ramble 5) came here to fish in what he called 'the loveliest of vale rivers', and also wrote part of The Water Babies *while staying in the village. Kingsley may well have seen the rebuilding of St John's in 1863. All that remains of the earlier Norman church are the chancel arch and the ornamental stone over the porch doorway. The timber framing of the barrel vaulted roof is an impressive example of Victorian craftsmanship.*

In the shade of the venerable churchyard yew tree lies John Hughes, a gypsy sentenced to death at Winchester Assizes in 1825 for horse stealing, the last man to be hanged for this offence in England. Due to the forgiving nature of the then Rector, Robert Wright, who owned the horse, the body was buried in consecrated ground.

3 Facing lych-gate, take track to right and shortly enter enclosed path beside meadows sloping down to the River Itchen. A series of swing-gates now marks the path ahead, in sight of the river, eventually to reach lane at Chilland.

There is an intriguing tradition that the Danes built boats on the banks of the Itchen and that their word

First glimpse of the River Itchen

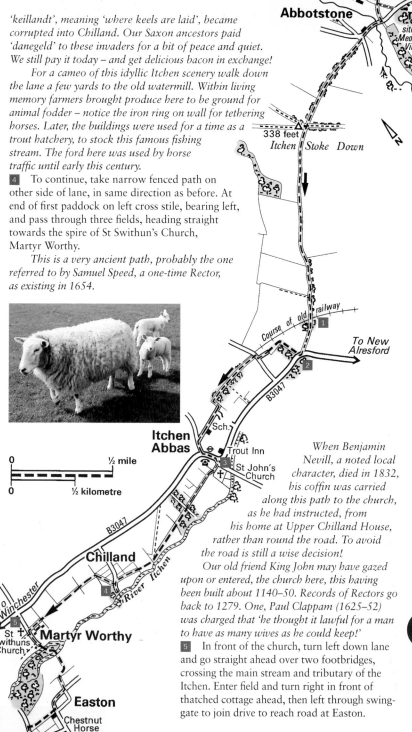

'keillandt', meaning 'where keels are laid', became corrupted into Chilland. Our Saxon ancestors paid 'danegeld' to these invaders for a bit of peace and quiet. We still pay it today – and get delicious bacon in exchange!

For a cameo of this idyllic Itchen scenery walk down the lane a few yards to the old watermill. Within living memory farmers brought produce here to be ground for animal fodder – notice the iron ring on wall for tethering horses. Later, the buildings were used for a time as a trout hatchery, to stock this famous fishing stream. The ford here was used by horse traffic until early this century.

[4] To continue, take narrow fenced path on other side of lane, in same direction as before. At end of first paddock on left cross stile, bearing left, and pass through three fields, heading straight towards the spire of St Swithun's Church, Martyr Worthy.

This is a very ancient path, probably the one referred to by Samuel Speed, a one-time Rector, as existing in 1654.

When Benjamin Nevill, a noted local character, died in 1832, his coffin was carried along this path to the church, as he had instructed, from his home at Upper Chilland House, rather than round the road. To avoid the road is still a wise decision!

Our old friend King John may have gazed upon or entered, the church here, this having been built about 1140–50. Records of Rectors go back to 1279. One, Paul Clappam (1625–52) was charged that 'he thought it lawful for a man to have as many wives as he could keep!'

[5] In front of the church, turn left down lane and go straight ahead over two footbridges, crossing the main stream and tributary of the Itchen. Enter field and turn right in front of thatched cottage ahead, then left through swing-gate to join drive to reach road at Easton.

14

Turn right and follow road round left-hand bend into the village. With Chestnut Horse just ahead, turn right into narrow fenced path beside the pub. Cross stile into field and with fence on left, bear right of farm buildings to stile in front of cottages. Turn left along road and then shortly right, into Church Lane.

1 Beyond the Church of St Mary, and the Old School House, turn right through gate into one-time school field. Go diagonally across this meadow and on same line down through next field to reach river. Keep to right-hand side of the fields ahead, finally becoming a wooden-railed path, leading under motorway. On other side of M3, follow right-hand wooden fence where it turns sharp right. Soon, you are once again following the Itchen.

On reaching a drive, the right of way to the right affords an excellent opportunity, given the time, to enjoy again the river scenery; a series of footbridges carry the path from the nearby pretty Fulling Mill cottage, over a labyrinth of streams to reach the villages of Kings Worthy, Abbots Worthy and even Headbourne Worthy – all very Worth-while!

2 Continue along the riverside path, following fringe of trees on right. Where Easton Down sweeps up to left, carrying its noisy burden, follow the twisting path down to and under two road bridges (the first with limited headroom – duck or grouse!) After a narrow woodland section, cross stile to follow right-hand side of long meadow to stile and continue in wide grass strip. Finally leave fields at stile, and head along tarmac farm track leading to Easton Lane.

3 Here turn right, as the road becomes Wales Street and about 100 yards after aptly–named hostelry, First In – Last Out, turn right between Nos. 11 & 13 to continue in same direction, now on riverside path. Stay close to stream, along the gardens of Water Lane, to pass the Youth Hostel (part of Town Mill, National Trust), at junction with Bridge Street. You are now in the heart of Winchester; for centuries the capital of Saxon England.

Carefully cross road, turn right and immediately beyond 18th-century St Swithun's Bridge, turn left down steps to The Weirs. Within a few yards notice plaque recording the only visible section of the city's Roman wall.

Where path ahead divides, fork right and soon right again, following the impressive flint wall of Wolvesley Castle, *built in 1138 by Henry de Blois, Bishop of Winchester, but reduced to a shell in the Civil War.*

4 Continue ahead along College Street passing Winchester College, the famous public school. *Founded in 1382 by William of Wykeham, the school motto is well known: 'Manners makyth Man'. But not so polite is the Latin inscription on one of the old buildings. This translates as 'Learn, Leave or be Licked'!*

At end of College Street turn right through Kingsgate, or more fully: 'St Swithun upon Kingsgate'. This tiny medieval church, first mentioned in 1263/4, is built over the arches. Immediately turn right again, through another gateway, into The Close with the exceptionally beautiful houses of Cheney Court immediately on right. At end of building on left, bear left towards the Cathedral, and pass under flying buttresses (a necessary 20th-century addition) to reach the West Door.

This masterpiece of medieval masonry was moulded together in various architectural styles during the 450 years from 1079. King Henry III was baptised here, Richard the Lion Heart was crowned here, Queen Mary I was married here, Jane Austen and Izaak Walton are buried here. Truly a treasure house of English history.

5 With your back to the Cathedral door, walk diagonally across the Square, shortly passing under covered way to reach and turn left up High Street. At top, in front of Westgate, turn left up Castle Hill, finally to reach the hilltop site of Winchester Castle and, across the cobbled yard, the splendid medieval Great Hall.

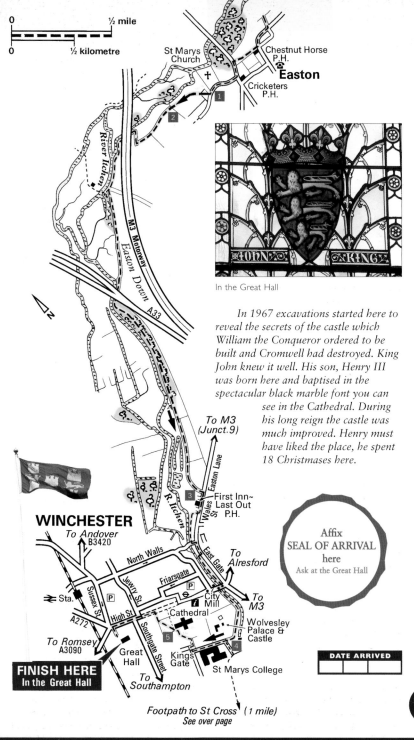

0 ½ mile
0 ½ kilometre

St Marys Church

Chestnut Horse P.H.

Easton

Cricketers P.H.

[1]

[2]

River Itchen

M3 Motorway

Easton Down

A33

N

In the Great Hall

In 1967 excavations started here to reveal the secrets of the castle which William the Conqueror ordered to be built and Cromwell had destroyed. King John knew it well. His son, Henry III was born here and baptised in the spectacular black marble font you can see in the Cathedral. During his long reign the castle was much improved. Henry must have liked the place, he spent 18 Christmases here.

To M3 (Junct. 9)

Easton Lane

R. Itchen

[3]

Wales St

First Inn~ Last Out P.H.

WINCHESTER

To Andover B3420

North Walls

To Alresford

Jewry St

Friarsgate

East Gate

To M3

Sta.

Sussex St

P

P

City Mill

A272

High St

Cathedral

Wolvesley Palace & Castle

To Romsey A3090

[5]

Southgate Street

Kings Gate

[4]

Great Hall

St Marys College

FINISH HERE
In the Great Hall

To Southampton

Footpath to St Cross (1 mile)
See over page

See over page

Affix
SEAL OF ARRIVAL
here
Ask at the Great Hall

DATE ARRIVED

15

. . . and now for the Wayfarer's Dole ▶

St Cross, from the quadrangle

Given the time and energy, a fitting conclusion to this Three Castles walk, is to follow our old friend 'Itchen Streeme' for just one more mile, through the water-meadows south of the city to St Cross. Here you may still knock at the Porter's Lodge to claim the Wayfarer's Dole – a 'horn' of ale and some bread – once provided for 100 poor men every day.

The Hospital of St Cross and Almshouse of Noble Poverty, to give it its full title, has been described as 'the finest and grandest surviving almshouse of the Middle Ages in England still serving the original purpose'. St Cross was founded in 1136 by Henry de Blois, Bishop of Winchester (the Conqueror's grandson) to provide a safe haven for thirteen elderly gentlemen. In the 15th century a new foundation was set up – the Almshouse of Noble Poverty – to provide for 'those who had once had everything handsome about them, but had losses'. Since then 27 brethren have occupied the terrace of tall chimneyed houses built in 1446 along one side of the quadrangle.

St Cross is reached by retracing our steps past Winchester College, then turning right to follow the signposted route along College Walk and the riverside gravel path. Finally, bear right through field in front of the unmistakable medieval buildings, to enter Britain's oldest charitable institution.

If you have journeyed with us on foot these many miles from Windsor, we think you can fairly claim a little hospitality. Savour the Wayfarer's Dole!

PATH GRADIENT PROFILE

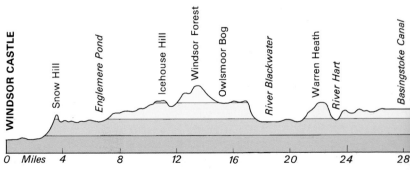

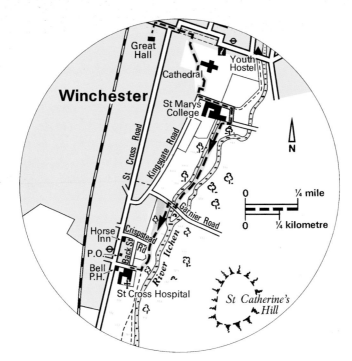

Contact addresses for footpath matters:

WINDSOR to Stage 3 (North of A329)
Royal Borough of Windsor and Maidenhead,
Highways Department, Town Hall, St Ives Road, Maidenhead SL6 1RF

Stage 3 (South of A329) to Stage 5 (River Blackwater)
Bracknell Forest Borough Council,
Leisure Department, Easthampstead House, Town Square, Bracknell RG12 1AQ

Stage 5 (River Blackwater) to WINCHESTER
Hampshire County Council,
Public Rights-of-Way Department, Mottisfont Court, High Street, Winchester SO23 8UD

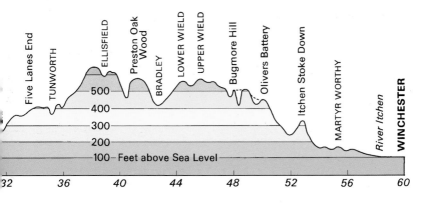

This circular walk in the western part of Windsor Great Park includes impressive distant views of Windsor Castle and the opportunity to visit the Copper Horse, with fine vistas down the Long Walk. Please observe the Regulations displayed at entrances to the Park.

Distance: about 4 miles

Start: Parking area on Sheet Street Rd (A332) opposite Cranbourne Gate (Grid ref. 947727).

With back to main road and Cranbourne Gate, follow narrow tarmac road with fenced field on left and woodland of Great Park on right, to reach, at top of rise, the red-brick Cranbourne Tower.

The Tower is the oldest building in the Park, thought to have been built about 1500. Samuel Pepys and John

Ted Green (English Nature) cataloging ancient oaks in the Great Park

Evelyn both record having stayed here in 1665 and 1673 respectively, in those days a much larger property. Most of it was demolished in 1861, retaining one large room at least, used by Queen Victoria during her carriage drives around the Park. On 3 May 1764 a horse was foaled here during a solar eclipse. Appropriately named Eclipse, the foal was to become one of the most famous racehorses of all time, being unbeaten in its 18 races.

1 From the sign 'Crown Estate – Private', retrace your steps some 65 yards and fork left across grass to follow minor paths through woodland, keeping paling fence close on left. (A bridle route runs parallel on right.) On reaching broad crossing track with field beyond, look for distant view of Windsor Castle. Turn right along track and in about 80 yards merge with sandy bridleway, to continue in same direction, keeping fence nearby on left.

Follow this bridleway, through left-hand bend, along edge of woodland. On emerging from trees turn right on grass path, along edge of woodland at first, then on tarmac drive, to main road.

Between here and our starting point at Cranbourne Gate, some 13 acres were planted with oaks in 1580. Many of these can still be seen.

2 With care cross main road and about 30 yards after entering Ranger's Gate, fork left on bridleway, climbing past woodland, then descending with fenced field on left. Towards bottom of slope bear right onto grass track which soon rejoins bridleway to pass beside Russell's Pond. Carry on for a short distance before bearing right beside avenue of oaks (re-planted 1995) – Queen Anne's Ride – shortly to reach road.

Queen Anne's Ride was first laid out in 1703, one of several rides cut through the Park to facilitate the Queen's enthusiasm for following her Buckhounds. At that time this particular ride led directly to the Royal Kennels, built by the Queen at Swinley Bottom, adjoining Ascot Heath.

3 Turn left along road and just beyond gate into Deer Park, bear right up narrow path beside bridleway. Where fence on right turns right, follow bridleway straight on across open strip, then between scattered trees, soon reaching the Copper Horse – the statue of King George III overlooking the Long Walk.

The Long Walk. In 1682 a warrant was issued for the purchase of land 'to make an avenue 240 ft wide between our Castle of Windsor and the Great Park there'. (See stages 1 & 2).

4 Turning your back to the Castle, walk away from the statue, soon descending to pass through gate in deer fence into broad hedged grass ride. *The pink-washed building amongst trees is Royal Lodge, used by the Queen Mother as a country retreat after she and the Duke of York first moved there in 1934.*

After just over 200 yards, turn right into another ride (closed to horses) leading to road ahead. Here turn left along the grass verge as far as the crossroads (known as Timber Cross) before turning right to reach houses at edge of The Village.

This model village was started in 1948 when 32 houses and a general stores & post office were built. Further houses were added in 1954 and 1966.

5 Follow the road over Queen Anne's Ride and past the recreation ground opposite the shop (an opportunity, perhaps, to purchase refreshments!). After pond on left, turn right at crossroads and at further crossroads, by sign: 'The Prince Consort Drive 1860', turn left along road to return to start.

DATE WALKED		

Tom Green's Field and Silwood Park

This circular walk follows footpaths and tracks in the historic parish of Sunninghill, where it is still possible to take a quiet country walk between the fingers, as it were, of an increasingly built-up area.

Distance: 4 miles

Start: Car park at eastern end of Ascot High St (A329) – free for public use except on race-days (Grid ref. 926688).

From car park carefully cross High St turning left to follow footway. Turn first right into St George's Lane and follow road round left-hand bend, to pass St George's School.

Notice the Victorian building, (once called St James's School), which the young Winston Churchill knew well as a prep-school boarder here in 1882/4 – apparently he hated it! Today it is a girl's school.

1 Continue down gravel track and at bottom of slope turn sharp right (Wells Lane). Soon pass sports ground – the area on left along here used to be known as Sunninghill Bog but now, cleared and drained, it is put to more productive uses, hence the current name – St George's Fields.

Bear left at junction of byways and pass under railway arch to reach St George's Lane. Turn left, then immediately fork left along tarmac path with wooden fence to gardens on right. Pass through second barrier and turn left along Lower Village Rd, under railway bridge. Shortly, after several properties on left, turn left into Coombe Lane. Some 50 yards beyond last big house on right, Coombe Grange, turn right into Tom Green's Field – a picnic area. *This name commemorates a late chairman of the Parish Council, during whose term of office in the 1970s, the field was purchased to preserve it from development.*

2 Follow the middle path through light woodland, past tennis courts on right and then along track to left of Victory Field – a memorial to the men who lost their lives in WW1. *This field was landscaped 'by hand' during the depression of the 1920s, when the men were paid 6d per hour.*

At main road cross carefully, turning left along footway. At end of wall turn right into narrow path alongside garden of Wellsbridge Cottage, leading to T-junction of paths.

Shady path near St Michael's Church

Before turning right at this point, it is an interesting diversion to turn left for some 150 yards to cross Hog Brook, notable for its perpetual brown colour, caused by algae. Beyond the stream, away to the right across parkland, stands the renovated Tetworth Hall. Now retrace your steps straight back along this path soon to reach St Michael's Church.

The Parish Church we see today was restored in 1824 but there has been one on this site since 1199. The remarkable hollow yew tree, with its iron girdle, is claimed to be over 1000 years old.

3 Walk through the churchyard, with its ornate monuments and into the lane leading around the church. Pass the burial ground, go through a kissing gate and along a wide strip between fields – known as Church Path. At bottom of slope, pass kissing gate and go up slowly rising path with glimpses of Silwood Lake away to left. A few yards beyond high metal gate on right (private path to Silwood Park), turn left along narrow enclosed path.

Silwood Park is today a Field Station for Imperial College of Science and Technology. The timber-framed old building to left of path here is the one-time farmhouse and barn of Silwood Park estate.

4 Exit onto roadside by well preserved kissing and carriage gates, the latter complete with unusual latch. Cross over (Cheapside Rd), turning left along footway. Cross end of Watersplash Lane and then over driveway to Sunninghill Park, at East Lodge. (For interesting details about this particular spot see end of Stage 2.) Where road forks, by Silwood Park Nurseries, bear left, shortley to reach the impressive Golden Gates. At end of railings to left of gates, turn right into enclosed path alongside racecourse. At junction with road (A330 Winkfield Rd) turn left to return to start.

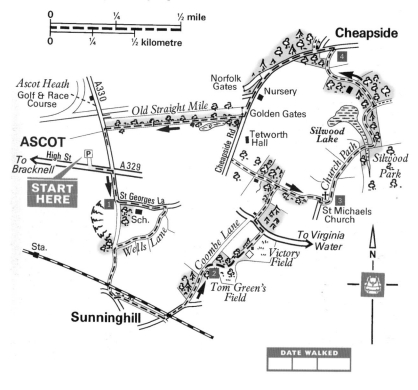

Heathlake and Gorrick Woods

This easy, gentle circular walk takes full advantage of the woods and forest remaining on the northern fringe of the much developed village of Crowthorne, and includes the seven-acre lake set in the 50 acres of wooded Heathlake Park, now in the care and protection of Wokingham District Council.

Distance: about 4 miles
(2 mile alternative)

Start: Small car park at Heathlake Park, off Nine Mile Ride (Grid ref. 828653).

Facing Heathlake, follow path from car park beside lake on left, soon bearing left between tall trees, still with lake nearby. At footbridge (do not cross), turn right along tarmac path for a few yards. Continue ahead on broad grass strip for 80 yards before turning right along estate path between gardens. Shortly cross road, pass to right of No. 24 and continue in same direction. At

T-junction turn right along broad tree-lined path (Oaklands Lane). Reaching golf course carefully cross fairway into tree-lined path ahead. Shortly, look for path turning right at end of wood, now with small playing field on left.

1 Join tarmac path to Ravenswood Village – a charitable foundation caring for adults and children with learning difficulties. Please keep dogs on leads through this area. On reaching main drive, turn left along it. Soon notice building with small clock pinnacle, above rose garden. This contains an attractive café and mini-market, open to passers-by. Where drive divides, keep straight on along track and turn right onto narrow path leading behind stables. Eventually, where this grassy path forks, keep left, shortly to reach roadside. FOR SHORTER WALK take right fork and follow woodland path ahead (with road nearby on left) back to car park at start.

2 To continue longer walk carefully cross road, opposite Kingsbridge

Winter at Heath Lake

Cottages, turning right along footway soon reaching the quaintly named Who'd a Tho't It. Turn left along grassy path on left side of pub, leading to playing field, with its splendid sports pavilion (St Sebastians Playing Field Trust). Turn left across near corner of playing field, pass through gap in hedge and turn sharp right along edge of woodland (part of Bramshill Forest). At path junction, where playing field on right ends, turn left along broad track. At next path junction continue ahead and at end of this section bear right, still on broad forest track. This track soon straightens, gently descending at first.

3 At low wooden posts across track, continue on into narrower path. A house comes into view away on left (Gorrick Cottage) after which, at T-junction, turn right to pass metal gate. Stay on this track to leave finally, at wooden posts – Gorrick Woods.

4 Cross road ahead and continue in same direction along byway (Hatch Ride), soon passing Heathlands Riding Centre on right. Beyond here the road shrinks to a path, soon reaching busy road near roundabout. Here turn sharp right along tarmac footway. Where this joins roadside, cross carefully to re-enter Heathlake Park by stile in boundary fence. Within a few yards, turn right for 25 paces, and then left (in front of white post) for 30 paces. Here, at T-junction, turn right and within a few yards bear left onto wider path, soon descending gently, still through trees. At bottom of slope, on reaching path junction, turn right and follow path through trees with lake on left, leading back to car park at start.

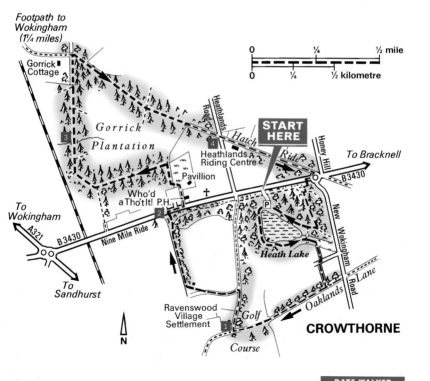

Blackwater Valley and Spout Pond

This circular walk crosses varied countryside between the Blackwater River and the delightful National Trust and adjoining mixed woodland of Finchampstead Ridges.

Distance: about 4 miles

Start: Car park at Ambarrow Court Countryside Park (Grid ref. 825626). Also easily accessible by footpath from Crowthorne Station (see map Stage 5).

From car park entrance carefully cross road (A321) and pass through stile-way into footpath along edge of woodland strip. Joining road ahead, within a few yards turn left into field through wooden swing-gate. Follow ditch along edge of two fields, passing buildings of Ambarrow Farm away to right. At end of second field cross lane with kissing gates either side into meadow where gravel path leads ahead through a water sports centre beside Horseshoe Lake. Beyond the launching area stay on gravel path, finally bearing right in front of one swing-gate, to shortly reach a second. Here turn right along path beside River Blackwater, the boundary between Berkshire and Hampshire.

You are now in the Blackwater Valley, which extends some 12 miles between Eversley and Aldershot, along the Hampshire border with Berkshire and Surrey. Since 1979 the Local Authorities and others have been developing facilities for a wide range of activities in the valley, including walking, boating, fishing, etc.

1 Follow the riverside path for nearly a mile with pleasant vistas across the lakes towards the wooded hills of Finchampstead. But be sure, at the end of Horseshoe Lake to turn left through swing-gate to stay beside the river. On reaching wooden bridge over Blackwater, continue along same bank, on right-hand of two paths ahead. Path shortly turns right, away from river. Soon cross bridleway bridge and immediately fork right on gravel path, past access gate to nearby hide. At end of path cross car park and turn left (Lower Sandhurst Rd) Take first turning on right, Dell Road, and just beyond

Near Beech Hill

second property, South Ridge, turn right at wooden barrier into National Trust woodland of Finchampstead Ridges. Follow raised footpath between bridleway and ditch. Where path rises go straight on, soon descending to pass to right of Spout Pond.

Finchampstead Ridges is one of the National Trust's earliest acquisitions. The first 60 acres of woodland were purchased by public subscription in 1913 for £3,000, part of the Bearwood estate owned by Mr John Walter, a Berkshire MP and proprietor of the Times *newspaper. In 1863 Mr Walter had constructed the road over The Ridges and planted the Wellingtonia Avenue, still a splendid sight today. In more recent years, gifts of adjoining woodland have increased the acreage to 138, with over 60*

species of birds recorded.

2 After Spout Pond continue up slope, turning right past barrier, then left up rising gravel drive, shortly passing Rourke's Drift (beware of Zulus!) At top of incline by deep ditches, turn right along woodland path and where gap in trees on right gives glimpse of view, bear left along path which soon descends steeply into gully. Way continues along enclosed path with field on right sweeping up towards the fine wooded knoll of Beech Hill.

3 At green field gate on right, path widens into gravel track bearing left to reach road opposite one-time Ambarrow Farm. Turn left along road, passing Ambarrow Lodge. Where road turns left, our circuit is complete, so continue ahead on footpath back to start.

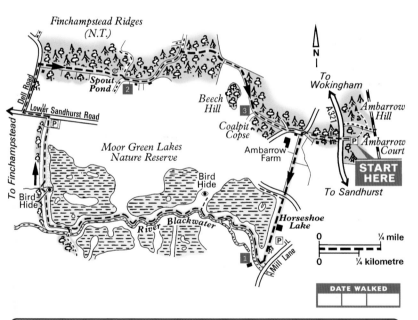

Although few signs remain today of the house, Ambarrow Court was a substantial Victorian mansion built on this site in 1885 by a Col. Harvey, whose widow lived here until her death in 1932, when the property was sold. In her will, Mrs Harvey left the adjoining Ambarrow Hill, some 14 acres of woodland, to the National Trust. So far, all efforts to discover the origins of this conical-shaped hill have failed. It is not believed, as might be supposed, to be man-made. A footpath from the corner of the car park leads directly to the summit.

This circular walk follows paths and tracks through a variety of Forestry Commission woodland on Heath Warren. It then visits the focal point of old Eversley, the historic Church and former Rectory, closely associated with the Victorian writer and social commentator, Charles Kingsley, who was Rector here for over thirty years.

Distance: about 3 miles

Start: Small parking area at entry to Forestry Commission woodland, junction of unclassified road with south end of St Neots Rd – about 1 mile west of Eversley Cross and 1 mile east of Bramshill (Grid ref. 766614).

With back to road, pass beside barrier and after 60 yards on gravel track, fork right along narrow winding path which rises slowly before running along right-hand side of mature woodland. Shortly, at prominent junction of five paths, turn right, down dip and up other side. About 50 yards beyond where track joins from left, turn left on waymarked path through mixed plantation, towards taller trees ahead.

The mature woodland in this part of Heath Warren, mainly Scots Pines, was planted in 1929. It is now fully grown and is being felled and replanted over a period, in accordance with a careful conservation plan. The opportunity has been taken to reopen part of Eversley Footpath 7 which was obscured by Scots Pines. New planting has provided a wider selection of trees, including Douglas Fir, Sweet Chestnut, and Cherry.

1 Continue ahead to join wide track along edge of forest – opposite small gravel lake. An ancient burial mound or tumulus lies immediately to the left at this point – Cudbury Clump. After 50 yards, and a similar distance before pylon ahead, bear left back into the forest, along slowly rising bridleway (Welsh Drive) for nearly a mile – ignoring turnings on both sides.

The younger trees along Welsh Drive, Scots Pine, Corsican Pine and some Birch were planted about 1970, after extraction of sand and gravel had reduced the ground level on the Heath by several feet.

2 Where track reaches highest point at 5-way crossing (notice one-time viewpoint – periscope now required!),

Welsh Drive

take first turning left along narrower path, with trees both sides. Follow track into mature woodland, before merging with slightly sunken track, soon with field on right. At bottom of woodland turn right between ornamental iron gate-posts and follow lane to pass house with ha-ha in front (the Old Rectory), before St Mary's Church. Notice here the Old Manor and Church Farm, where delightful old barns continue to serve a useful purpose.

Hopefully the Church will be open, as it is well worth a visit. Most of the present building was erected between 1724 and 1735, to designs by John James, one-time Surveyor to St Paul's Cathedral, who also built Warbrook House for himself, nearby in the village. Possible evidence of heathen worship on this site is the large sarsen stone which can be seen below the floorboards near the font. The most famous Rector here was Charles Kingsley – writer, teacher, academic, but essentially a caring parish priest, best remembered today perhaps as the author of The Water Babies.

There are memorials to him and his family in the Church, and he is buried close to the churchyard wall adjoining the Elizabethan house, which was the Rectory until 1971. Kingsley planted the Irish Yew trees lining the path to the porch. Soon after his death in 1875, his daughter planted a seed she and her father had brought back from the United States, of the enormous Sequoia in the middle of the churchyard. His grave bears the inscription: 'Amavimus, Amamus, Amabimus' – 'We loved, We love, We shall love'.

3 To continue the walk, follow path round back of Church, to leave churchyard through arch in yew hedge. Pass pond just visible through trees on right and after stile follow field-edge path ahead, through three fields with swing-gates. Then keep along edge of woodland with fine open views on right towards high ground on horizon. Driveway from left merges with path, along avenue of conifers. At meeting of forest tracks, bear right to return to start.

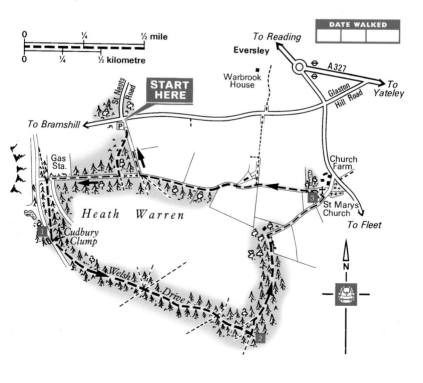

Broad Oak and the Bury

This circular walk passes through the fields and meadows which closely surround the ancient town of Odiham. Construction of the bypass in 1979 has restored the air of peace and prosperity that has endured here since its origin as a Saxon Royal Manor. Today it has the rare status of an Outstanding Conservation Area.

Distance: about 3¾ miles
Start: Odiham Wharf car park at Colt Hill (Grid ref. 747517). approached from London Road, Odiham

With your back to the bypass, walk to nearby towpath, close to red-brick Colt Hill Bridge which crosses the Basingstoke Canal here.

This was a busy wharf in the heyday of the canal. The old cottage by the bridge was once a public house and still retains its original name, the Cricketers. The Surrey & Hampshire Canal Society's boat, John Pinkerton (named after the engineer who built the canal) sometimes operates from here. (See Stage 8 for further canal details.)

1 Turn left along towpath, past boatyard on opposite bank (where holiday cruisers and day-boats can be hired in season). Go under bypass bridge and continue along canal bank to next bridge (Broad Oak). Pass under this bridge and after some 300 yards, where end of small lake (Wilks Water) meets canal, take narrow path branching left. At end of lake, look left to see, beyond white garden gates, an elegant little house with decorative brick gables, known today as King John's Hunting Lodge. It was built in 1730/40 as an ornament of nearby Dogmersfield Park and is now owned by the National Trust. (Not open to the public).

2 From a point about 25 yards in front of the white gates turn left into wood. Take left-hand of two minor paths which winds through the trees of Odiham Common, returning shortly to Broad Oak Bridge. Now cross bridge and soon join tarmac road ahead, with properties on right and green on left. At postbox outside Wincombe Cottage, turn left on gravel track. Pass between Greenwoods and Stream Cottage into short enclosed path, to cross sleeper bridge and rails into meadow. Here turn right and follow field boundary. Leave meadow in corner, to cross series of stiles, with stream close by on right, finally crossing stile next to drive from bungalow on left.

3 Carefully cross main road (A287), turn left down slope and after first property, turn right over stile and follow

Fishers Brook

hedge on right. Cross plank bridge over ditch, continue to end of hedge on right and then bear half-right to stile and wooden walkway over stream in corner of meadow. Now follow field-edge path ahead over one stile and through two left and right-hand turns, with wide views over fields to left. Keep hedge on right at all times until, eventually, from furthest corner of field, follow track bearing right, leading to road.

4 Within a few yards, turn left across road into Buryfields and immediately turn right to pass houses at roadside. Pass Odiham Cottage Hospital on left, then down slope to fork left along drive past Almshouses, to reach little old brick cottage straight ahead – the Pest House. Follow path down through churchyard, past the brick and flint west front of All Saints' Church.

The Almshouses and Pest House were built about 1625, the latter to house sufferers from the Plague and other infectious diseases – today it serves as a tiny museum in the care of the Odiham Society. The brick tower of All Saints was completed in 1649 on a 14th-century base. The four pinnacles were added in the 1800s. Hopefully you will have time and opportunity to admire the splendours (the modern stained glass, for instance) and curiosities of this historic building. In fact the whole town is worth a leisurely exploration.

Take the church path down into the Bury, the square in front of the church, and notice the old stocks and whipping post. Facing the Bell, turn right to pass between white posts and then turn left into narrow walled passage to right of the Tudor Stoney Cottage. Cross High Street and pass along right side of the George (first licensed in 1510). Immediately in front of the arched, red-brick Coach House, turn left through trellis arch then right, on gravel path. Follow narrow path between gardens and cross stile into open meadows stretching away in front.

5 Bear slightly left to cross ditch to right of two trees on first field boundary and then continue on same line through two more fields ahead, once part of a medieval royal park. At top of third field, cross two stiles and follow left-hand fence. Leave field by stile to right of metal gate, cross canal bridge and immediately turn right to follow canal bank back to Colt Hill Bridge and car park.

DATE WALKED

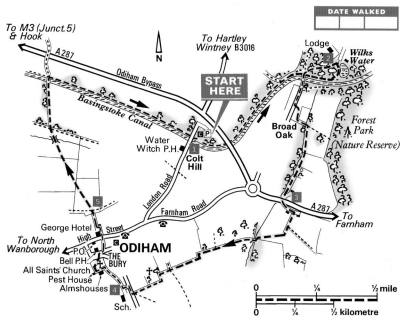

Travel Information

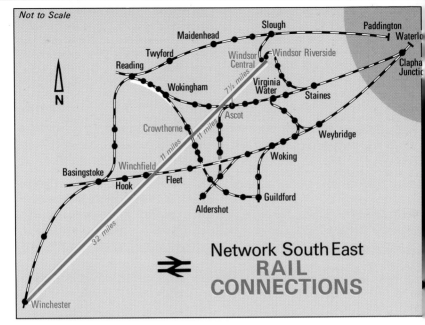

Network South East
RAIL CONNECTIONS

TRAIN SERVICES
For information on fares and timetables ring National Rail Enquires, Tel: **0345 484 950** (24-hour service, local call rate)
Approximate rail travelling times:
London (Paddington) to **Windsor** (via Slough) 30 minutes
London (Waterloo) to **Ascot** 53 minutes
Winchester to **London** (Waterloo) 1 hour 30 minutes
Winchester to **Reading** (via Basingstoke) 45 minutes
Reading to **Windsor** (via Slough) 35 minutes

BUS SERVICES
Bus services in the **Windsor, Ascot, Bracknell** and **Crowthorne** areas are currently operated mainly by the Berks Bucks Bus Company (The Bee Line). For detailed information contact the Bracknell Bus Station Travel Office, Tel: **(01344) 424938**
Open: Mon – Fri 09.00 – 17.15
       Sat 09.00 – 13.00
A map showing all the Bus and Rail services in **Hampshire** is obtainable from: The Passenger Transport Group, County Surveyor's Dept., Hampshire County Council, The Castle, Winchester, Hants SO23 8UD

For information (during office hours only) telephone: **(01962) 868944** or if phoning from within Hampshire **dial 100** and ask for Freephone County Bus Line.

TAXIS
If a situation should arise where a taxi would be useful, you can always telephone Talking Pages on freephone **0800 600 900**. The operator will give you details of two or three local car-hire services. These are currently available from **Yateley, Eversley, Hartley Wintney, Odiham** and **Alton**, as well as the larger towns.

MAPS
The following large scale Ordnance Survey 1:25,000 Explorer maps highlight the route of the Three Castles Path and also show additional topographical detail in the area:
132 Winchester; 144 Basingstoke;* 159 Reading; 160 Windsor*
Also cover the six circular walks.